# THE WORDS WE NEVER PLAN TO SAY

*Leanne Ayse*

# TRIGGER WARNING

This book is an approximation of the night I was sexually assaulted. Reader discretion is advised. This is not a one hundred percent accurate retelling of events. This was written to be a cathartic experience for me as a survivor and while I'm choosing to share it with you I am asking that you keep that in mind as you open these pages. I felt it was important to share my story because sexual assault looks different for everyone and I think a lot of people forget that. To all the other survivors out there, I see you and I believe you.

If you have any questions you can email me at LeanneAlyseAuthor@gmail.com \

LEANNE ALYSE

To the ASSHOLE with the small dick who thought I was weak. I'm not. Fuck you. Also, I lied, five inches isn't average and even if it was, you were definitely smaller, and THANK THE GODS for that.

LEANNE ALYSE

# PLAYLIST

Emails I Can't Send – Sabrina Carpenter

    I Hate It Here – Taylor Swift

    Lie to Girls – Sabrina Carpenter

    The Smallest Man Who Ever Lived – Taylor Swift

    Til It Happens To You – Lady Gaga

    Would've, Could've, Should've – Taylor Swift

    when the party's over – Billie Eilish

LEANNE ALYSE

# A BAD KISS AND A
# CHEAP BOTTLE OF RED

F ebruary was always a month that I hated. I hate it more now. Valentine's Day is a drag when you don't have a date or someone to share it with and the month itself is nonsense in the way it's counted. Why do I have to remember if it's a leap year or not? Just pick how many days you want and shut up.

I knock on his apartment door, my toes curling in my boots as I push up and down on them waiting for him to answer. My red dress is cute enough to be putting in effort but not scantily clad that it makes it seem like I'm trying to get laid. But I am... I am trying to get laid.

My sexual awakening was right about at seventeen and for the first year of that I was in a long distance relationship that was the definition of a disaster. After I finally broke that off and lost my virginity to someone else, I found out about a month later the fucker was cheating on me and gave me chlamydia, luckily treatable, thank god. And after that disaster one would think I'd never want to have sex again but I decided the only way out is through, so fuck the trauma I want to know what good sex is like.

Which is how I found myself here, at nineteen, outside of the apartment of a man I've only ever met online and who I'm really fucking hoping won't kill me.

Please don't kill me.

He opens the door and I quickly take in the man smirking at me like I'm the hottest thing he's seen in his life. He's in his thirties, soft but perfectly kept scruff across his face that hadn't begun to gray yet like some of my other recent conquests. His features are... soft, not rugged like I was hoping for or sharp, more rounded. He runs a hand through his short hair and steps aside to let me in the door.

"Hi." He smiles.

Please, please don't kill me.

"Hi." I smile back, trying to walk in with a confidence that is most definitely fake, not that he knows that. I swagger through the door and up the stairs like I've been here before and this is my place not his, really I'm just trying to put some distance between his burning hot glare at myself, and the stairs are the only way to go.

As I get to the top I notice him following behind me and most definitely looking up my skirt. Fine by me, I made my intentions fairly clear in our messages, stupid? Maybe, but I knew what I wanted.

His place is about the same size as my apartment, honestly my place may be a little bigger. Not that size matters... no sorry. It totally does.

The stairway led up to a living room that opened into a kitchen. The bathroom is behind the kitchen and the bedroom behind the living room. The place is painted a stark white that seems plain but honestly, so is the mocha couch and the black coffee table.

"Shoes off." He tells me. I do and then he puts his hand on the small of my back and leads me into the kitchen. "Wine?" He purrs.

I chuckle. "Trying to get me drunk?"

He shrugs. "We'll see where the night takes us."

I stand beside him as he opens a bottle of red. I know next to nothing about which types of red are which but I know I like red over white and that's the important part. What I really like is tequila, but I think asking for that would be a little tacky.

"It's just a blend, but," He puts his thumb under my chin and tilts my head up to look at him, "It should still be perfect for what we need."

I nod as he leans down and presses a kiss to my lips and it... sucks. Fuck. Do not fucking tell me I came all this way for sex and this man is a fucking dud. Given it wasn't that far but, a half hour? That's still a long ways to drive for *bad* sex. For good sex, I'd drive an hour... more. Yeah, I'd drive more.

He kisses like a sloppy dog and it's grossing me the fuck out. His tongue isn't staying in his mouth or mine and when it does manage to find my mouth he doesn't seem to know what to do with it. How did this man make it to thirty kissing like this?

Because he's single that's why.

Yeah... should have considered that.

Wine. Wine will help. Both for him and me.

Besides, kissing doesn't really matter anyways. It's not a sign of anything except how oral would go and I've never really liked oral anyways. I like giving it, but receiving always feels so weird. I'm just laying there awkwardly while they lick around down there and then I have to pretend to moan so they don't get discouraged and yeah, we'll just try to avoid that tonight.

He pulls away after what feels like a small eternity and while I kind of already want to leave because a watermelon margarita in my own bed with my vibrator is slowly starting to sound like a better plan than what's his name, I don't want to be rude.

He pours the wine into two solo cups and passes me one of them. I take a sip of it and smile a little with a nod to let him know it's good when it absolutely is not. This shit is bitter as all hell.

He sets his drink down and his hands start running over my body in ways that feel much better than his kiss. "Let me run you a bath." He purrs, his hand cupping the swell of my ass.

I nod softly. "Yeah."

He turns me around spanking my ass softly as he sends me off into the bathroom with my solo cup of cheap wine and for a moment I dare to hope this night will turn out okay.

# An Uncomfortable Bath and a Questionable Edible

I push myself up onto the counter and pull my hair up into a ponytail as he runs the water. I'm more than sure of the fact that this is just an excuse to get me naked as quickly as possible so he can stare at my body, but honestly, I'm okay with that. I may not love my figure, but most men seem to appreciate it and I'm just glad to be wanted.

He plugs the drain and starts to fill the tub with the water, putting in some soap with it as he does. "You'll need to take off that dress." He whispers as he eyes me like he's trying to see what's underneath.

I don't hesitate, setting my cup down on the counter and pulling the dress up and over my head. I toss it to the side and slip out of my panties as best I can while still sitting on the counter.

He completely abandons the bath in favor of coming over to touch me. "What do you like?" He purrs.

I shrug, I've never really been asked that question before so hearing it throws me a little. "I don't know." I chew on my lip. "I like pretty much anything, but I've never tried anal."

"Do you want to?" He asks.

I shake my head. "No."

He frowns. "Bummer." He brushes some of the hair away from my face. "I bet that ass of yours would feel so good."

I shake my head again. "Off limits." I lean into him, "But I'm sure we can find a different hole of mine for you to fuck." I promise.

He nods optimistically. "I can understand having boundaries." He takes a step back from me and starts messing with the water again. "I've had mine not respected in the past."

"I'm sorry." I whisper.

He shrugs. "It was a long time ago." He shuts the water off now that the tub is mostly full. "I was raped when I was younger. I never truly felt like I got the power back after that."

My heart breaks in my chest. I'd never known someone that happened to and hearing him talk about it hit deeper than I can explain. There was a boy in high school that had spread my legs with his at the lunch table without my consent, but that was nothing compared to an actual assault. I don't know what to say so I just repeat the obvious. "I'm so sorry."

He turns and his eyes scan mine looking for something, but what I don't know. In the end he comes up to me and runs a hand through my hair. "It's not your fault, but thank you." He helps me off the counter and into the bathtub.

I relax into the water and do my best to try and work past the conversation we just had because I really don't want to dwell on that.

A silence fills the white tile bathroom as he stares at me. I take another sip of my wine and run my hand over the water softly. I don't know what to say to make this better. I don't know how to fix it and all I want to do is try and alleviate some of the tension in this room.

Right when I was about to try, he speaks again, "Do you want an edible?"

God yes. "Yeah, please."

He nods and starts fumbling through the bathroom cabinet. I take another sip of my wine zoning out and try to calm myself down because while I'm not sure if sex is or is not on the table now, I still have to either spend the rest of the night with this dude or figure out how to excuse myself. The latter sounds harder.

He takes the wine from me and passes me the edible. "Eat it and then take a big sip of the wine." He orders softly. His hand plays around the rim of the cup but I'm too busy with the edible to really think much of it, besides at this point I've had about half that glass of wine, I'm definitely tipsy. It doesn't take much for me to get a buzz going which is both a blessing and a curse.

He passes me back the glass and I drink some more of it down before passing it back to him. By now the water is starting to get cold and I'm just about shivering from the chill in the air.

"Do you want to get out?" He asks.

I nod and he helps me to my feet. "Let me get you a towel and then we can move to the couch." He purrs, his hand wrapping around the small of my back to help me step out of the tub. He pulls me in for another kiss and while I know nothing has changed, this one doesn't bother me as much. I'm probably just relaxed from the bath.

He pulls a towel off the shelf beside the sink and wraps it around me before leading me out of the bathroom.

To this day, I still don't like baths any-
more.

# A FAST RAPIST AND AN UNWANTED SEX ACT

He leads me over to the sofa to sit down, pulling me into his side. He strokes my hair softly. "Finish your drink." He orders.

I shake my head already feeling buzzed and out of it. "I..."

He takes the glass from me and puts it to my lips before slowly starting to tip the drink back. I cooperate because what the hell else am I supposed to do? I feel weak already, my bones mush from the edible that's kicking in faster than normal and the wine that I've been nursing all night.

"Good girl." He purrs as he sets the glass down on the coffee table and puts something on the TV that I have no hope of paying attention to in this state of fucked up.

I really didn't think I had that much. Maybe the edible was stronger than I thought. I don't fully understand what's happening, but I start dozing in and out of sleep, my mind completely unable to keep my body awake.

He shakes me softly. "Are you up?"

I nod feverishly, trying to get myself upright. "Yeah, I'm... I'm fine." I slur out.

He smirks a little but the expression is hazy. "Let's get you to bed." He helps me up to my feet and leads me towards his bedroom.

One second I remember being in the doorway the next I remember being face down on the bed. Standing autonomously wrapped in the towel... and then I wasn't. Then I was stuck. In a gap between time and space as I heard the bottle of lube pop open.

"Be grateful I'm using this." He growls, spreading my ass cheeks and rubbing a handful between the two of them.

"What?" I slur, trying to push myself over into a seated position, but my arms feel weak, my everything feels weak.

Two fingers push into my ass and I let out a cry that's quickly muffled by a hand clasping over my mouth. He shushes me and starts to massage at my ass with the two fingers, stretching me out.

I hear the squeak of the bed as he climbs on top of me and between my legs. He squirts a handful more lube so that it's dripping down my body and only then does he push at my asshole's entrance and start to shove his dick inside.

I let out another scream and this time he doesn't try to muffle it. I feel fully awake now in a way I didn't a few moments prior. Suddenly every nerve ending in my body is shocked as my asshole burns from the unwanted penetration.

I start crying into the mattress as he pushes fully inside and seats himself against my ass cheeks.

"Shhhh." He hushes me. "I'll be quick."

My eyes go wide at the words as I try to put together what's happening to me in this moment. I don't fully understand what's happening but I can feel the way my soul is getting stuck to this moment. Like a part of me is fraying away at the edges. Like a part of me will always be stuck in this room.

Seconds start to blur together but in a way that feels more like a small eternity is passing than like it's moving quickly. It's like every second is eating the others and no single moment in time will move forwards.

Just.

Move.

Forwards.

But I can't. Because all I can do is feel the way he's taking my ass and cry into the mattress, too out of it to truly be able to say anything coherent, too out of it to say anything at all.

God, this hurts so fucking much.

It's this uncomfortable pressure like I need to shit but I can't because I'm not controlling my body in this moment, he is.

He keeps going.

I just try to breathe through it. I try to keep myself going in that moment so I don't just all out fall apart. And for a moment I convince myself I'm somewhere else. I stare off into the distance and lose myself inside my mind, going numb to the world around me and blanking out everything.

Everything.

He grunts a few more times and despite his promise to be quick, he's not. He's taking fucking forever and all I want in the world is for him to just get the fuck off of me.

Finally, after prolonging my torture for god only knows how long, he presses himself into me and lets out a groan into my ear. "You felt so good, baby." He purrs to me as he pulls out and rolls over onto his back.

"See, that wasn't so bad." He brushes some of the hair away from my face as he pulls me into his arms. "And you said you didn't want it."

# A FAKE APOLOGY AND A BATHROOM BREAK

I don't understand. I would have done just about anything else this man wanted. Why did he take the one thing I wasn't okay with? The one thing I told him not to do?

I cry into his arms as he holds me in his bed. The white walls of the room spinning in circles around me as I try to put back together the shattered pieces of my mind and body.

I can feel his cum dripping out of my asshole.

He holds me and shushes me, telling me that it's alright. "I'm sorry." He whispers against my forehead as he presses a kiss to my temple. "I'm so sorry."

I don't have it in me to do anything but nod to the door to his bathroom. "I need... I... I have to..." I stumble over the words, I would just get up but he's holding me too tight. "I need to use the bathroom."

He helps me to my feet and guides me through the door and helps me down onto the toilet. "I have a bidet." He turns it down and it starts to rinse away his sins. Another bathroom item I still can't use to this day.

The bidet violates me in the same way that he did and takes away any proof I had of what he did to me, not that I had any hopes of doing anything with that proof anyways. I don't know where my purse is but I know I'm stuck here for the night with how fucked up I am.

"Does it feel like it's all out?" He asks me.

I nod, not knowing what else to do in this situation. How did I get here?

I know I wanted to have meaningless sex but this definitely wasn't what I had in mind. This was the last thing I had in mind.

I look at my clothes still crumpled on the bathroom floor and begin to sob into my hands.

He rubs my back and shushes me softly while I continue to cry. I'm ugly crying too, the kind with snot dripping all down my face and tears pouring out of my eyes. I'm drooling a little, but I really don't care. I don't know if I'll ever stop crying.

I feel so violated.

He grabs a wash cloth off the counter and passes it to me. I dry my face on it as best as I can, trying to calm myself down so I can just pee and be done with this. Eventually, I do pee and get up off the toilet on shaking legs. I stumble over to the sink and wash my hands quickly not wanting to be near the bidet a second longer although now that I think about it the other option is back to his bedroom and that seems worse.

He passes me back the wash cloth for my face before taking my other hand and pulling me back along into the bedroom. He guides me down into the bed and pulls the covers up around me comfortably before getting back in on the other side.

He pulls me into him once again and does his best to keep me quiet, I don't think that was for my own sake I think it had more to do with not wanting to wake his neighbors.

I sniffle as my mind tries to drift off to sleep but my body is still in shock. Has he done this to other women?

Why has he been so... caring and then he fucking... he... he... he raped me.

My mind starts replaying the whole night over trying to figure out where my misstep was, trying to figure out where I gave him a wrong signal or what I did that made this happen. I had to have done something wrong. I made a mistake somewhere, I just don't know what it is.

"I'm sorry." I whisper.

I shouldn't have gotten so fucked up. Clearly that wine and the edible did more than I thought they did and I should have known my limits.

I shouldn't have started crying. I'm clearly annoying him and I don't want to bug anyone with my sobbing. I'm such a fucking burden.

I shouldn't have come here.

I close my eyes as the world starts to darken around me... no, no, he just turned off the light, but I still did close my eyes. I can feel sleep trying to take me under as the fight or flight starts to wear off and everything begins to calm back down.

"You're okay." He whispers. "Just rest."

So I do.

# AN AWKWARD
# QUICKIE AND A
# DISSOCIATED DRIVE
# HOME

S unlight streams in through the sheer
curtains and I have no idea where the
fuck I am but I do know one thing for sure I
have a pounding fucking headache. A bone
deep exhaustion settles over me as I drift in
and out of sleep, but something inside of me
tells me I need to leave wherever this is.

When I finally get my eyes to stay open for
more than a couple seconds and see the man
next to me I gasp a little, then I look down
and realize I'm naked and pull the sheets up
over my body. Who?

Then all of last night comes rushing back
to me in a blur. Well, at least the parts
I can remember. The drink that he made

me finish, the way my mind seemed to drift in and out all night despite being physically awake, the fact that I shouldn't have been nearly that fucked up after one drink and an edible. I will never be able to prove it... but some part of my being just knows.

But then the worst image comes back to me, the one that haunts me for years to come and probably will for the rest of my life, him on top of me, in my ass. I remember my body pinned down to the bed by his weight and whatever was in my system. I remember him shoving himself inside me and me being too out of it to do anything about it except... survive.

"Oh fuck." I whisper, my eyes darting around the room like I'm actually taking it in for the first time. My phone is on the end table, my clothes are next to me on the floor despite that I definitely didn't put them there. Maybe I should burn that dress... I don't think I ever want to see it again, the panties too, burn them both and honestly while I'm at it maybe I could burn down this whole damned apartment with him inside.

That wouldn't be arson, it would be community service.

I'm about to get out of bed and try to sneak out of the room when I hear a groan from him. I freeze a little and turn my gaze to the man who fucking raped me and when I do I see him roll over to face me with a smile.

"Come here." He purrs, pulling me into him and I don't fight it because I'm a little scared of what would happen if I did. He presses another one of those awful fucking kisses to my lips and guides me back so I'm laying down on the bed. "Let me lick you."

Before I can answer one way or another he's moving himself under the covers and spreading my legs so he can go between them. I don't stop him, I don't say anything. I just stare at the ceiling and wait for whatever the hell he's about to do to me to be over so I can just go back home.

His tongue feels like sand paper between my legs and this feels worse than every other fucking time a guy has tried. He licks me while I sit there silently but I can tell he's getting annoyed. "Moan for me." He orders, giving another couple licks to my center.

I let out a moan that I thoroughly don't fucking feel and when I do he seems to recognize it for the fake that it is.

He spits between my legs and moves up to his knees. "How about I just fuck you instead?" But he's not really asking me because before I have a chance to answer he's slipping his cock between my legs, but at least this time he put it in my pussy instead of in my ass.

Small mercies I suppose.

I think sodomy would hurt a hell of a lot more if I wasn't fucked up as shit. Sex with a small dick feels like just about nothing, I can handle that sober.

I close my eyes and let my mind go back to the numb place between worlds. I try to let myself escape what he's doing to me and try to find somewhere quiet in the recesses of my mind to hide out for a little while, but then I hear his voice and feel his hand on my chin.

"Look at me." He growls.

My eyes pop open on command.

"Good girl." He keeps fucking into me as I try to control my breathing so I don't absolutely lose it. At least it sounds like panting so he can pretend in his mind I'm enjoying this while I pretend in mine to be anywhere fucking else.

I don't know how much time passes but eventually he pulls out of me and finishes across my stomach, another small mercy because while I have an IUD, I still don't want him cumming inside of me.

He cleans me up with the wash cloth that I was drooling snot into the night before and after a moment of laying there awkwardly I push up out of bed. I get dressed quickly and grab the rest of my shit before heading out towards the door.

He doesn't say anything to me as I close his bedroom door behind me. I take a deep breath on the other side of it before making a beeline to my shoes. I just carry them out with me, not wanting to stay in this damned god forsaken apartment a moment fucking longer.

I run down the stairs as fast as I can, doing my best not to cry until I get into my car, but when I finally close the car door behind me, I don't cry. I don't break down. I don't do anything but put the car in gear and disassociate my whole drive home.

# ACKNOWLEDGEMENTS

Thank you to you, the reader. I'm so sorry that I just put you through this but I appreciate you walking through the fires with me. At least this time, I wasn't alone.

Thank you to my husband for always helping me work through my trauma. This man may have scarred me but he fucked over my husband too because he was the one who put back together the pieces this asshole broke, but my husband has never once complained about that. He's always believed me and I needed someone who believed me when no one else did.

Thank you to everyone who believed me.

Fuck you to everyone who justified his actions.

Thank you to all the authors who came before me and inspired my works. Nothing is ever original and I'm okay with that. Where have I heard that before?

As always, thank you to typos. Withoot you I would be nothing. You make me the author I am today and I love you.

Finally, I want to thank God, because God gave me this book, and I feel God in this Chili's tonight.

# ABOUT THE AUTHOR

I'm bad at talking about myself but can write a 500 page book about someone else. Do with that information what you will.

As a kid I dreamed of being an author. I took a creative writing class in high school then proceeded to go on with my life and do nothing with it. That was until one day I decided to open a silly little document and start writing a silly little story about a healer and two kings who were in love with her. That cute little pet project that I thought would just be scrapped ten chapters in turned into a full blown trilogy that I'm more proud of than I can even explain.

I've always been a dreamer and sometimes if you keep your head in the clouds long enough, you do actually touch the stars.

I got married in September of 2024 to my loving husband. We had been together 4 years at that point and he's always encouraged me to go after what I'm passionate in. Finding that person who helps you achieve is so important and it's the best quality trait I could ask for in a partner.

Thanks for spending your time to read this. I hope you're having a great day and please make sure to check out my works. There's always more coming out. I'm one of those people who always has to be working on something so I promise you I am.

# CHECK OUT MY OTHER WORKS

<u>The Asher Series</u>
    Asher
    Burned
    Change


<u>A Literal Series Name</u>
A Cozy Airport Read
A Dark Romance Christmas


<u>Finally Writing My Memoirs</u>
The Words We Put on Our Tombstones
The Words We Never Plan to Say

LEANNE ALYSE

# The Siren and the Smoke Show

# CHECK OUT MY SOCIALS

Tiktok: @84Lele
Instagram: @the84Lele
Twitter: @84Lele84Lele
YouTube: @84Lele

www.ingramcontent.com/pod-product-compliance
Lightning Source LLC
Chambersburg PA
CBHW020346130626
46549CB00003B/1323